BEGINN
WITH TROPICALS

by **Diane Schofield**
Photos by Dr. Herbert R. Axelrod

Paul Hahnel, father of the fancy Guppy, has fish on his mind. Mr. Hahnel has devoted his whole life to fish.

The photographs on pages 7, 10, 11, 14, 15, 20, 22, 23, 27, 30, 34, 36, 37, 43, 44, 46, 47 are by Vincent Serbin.

Distributed in the U.S. by T.F.H. Publications, Inc., 211 West Sylvania Avenue, PO Box 427, Neptune, NJ 07753; in England by T.F.H. (Gt. Britain) Ltd., 13 Nutley Lane, Reigate, Surrey; in Canada to the pet trade by Rolf C. Hagen Ltd., 3225 Sartelon Street, Montreal 382, Quebec; in Canada to the book trade by H & L Pet Supplies, Inc., 27 Kingston Crescent, Kitchener, Ontario N28 2T6; in Southeast Asia by Y.W. Ong, 9 Lorong 36 Geylang, Singapore 14; in Australia and the South Pacific by Pet Imports Pty. Ltd., P.O. Box 149, Brookvale 2100, N.S.W. Australia; in South Africa by Valid Agencies, P.O. Box 51901, Randburg 2125 South Africa. Published by T.F.H. Publications, Inc., Ltd., the British Crown Colony of Hong Kong.

CONTENTS

Very fancy varieties of the common Platies and Swordtails are now available thanks to a housewife, Mrs. Thelma Simpson. She developed a Swordtail (lower fish) with an elongated dorsal fin. In short order professional breeders transferred the hifin to Platies (top fish).

The plain Black Molly has been equipped with a fancy tail and is now known as the "Lyretail Molly."

Introduction

If a poll were taken on the most commonly heard remarks made by people viewing an attractive tropical fish aquarium for the first time, the one winning the most tallies would be, "Oh, I'd love to have an aquarium if keeping tropical fish just weren't so complicated!" The ironic thing is that the people who make this statement have, in all probability, just come from behind the wheel of a car. Admittedly, an automobile is a rather involved bit of machinery, but once the basic ground rules have been learned, operating it no longer becomes a complicated voyage into the never-never land of confusion.

The same thing is true of keeping tropical fish. Once a few basic rules are learned, keeping a little bit of a tropical river in your home need not evoke any obscure fears nor make any mystical incantations necessary to help the small inhabitants of this transplanted river survive.

Tanks  1
A Lot

To most people on the brink of purchasing their first tropical fish tank, anything larger than a five gallon aquarium seems like something on which they could install a full-size diving board, leap in, and do the back stroke. When optical illusions are listed, an empty aquarium should go somewhere near the top of the list as appearing overwhelmingly larger than it actually is.

However, with no sleight of hand or juggling involved, it also seems to shrink as you find more and more to put in later on. Therefore, the cardinal rule on your first sally into learning a "fishy life" should be—BUY AT LEAST A TEN GALLON TANK. This message could well be embroidered in neat cross-stitches in a sampler to be hung on a prominent wall of your room.

Buy the largest aquarium you can afford; it will pay off with extra dividends of happiness for you, your children and the fish.

Hifin Wagtail Swordtails were one of the first products of Mrs. Simpson's famous Hifin Swordtail stock. Compare this to the pair of normal Wagtail Swordtails on the top of page 9.

A pair of Wagtail Swordtails. The male has the elongated tail. The Swordtail below is not called a Wagtail but a Berlin, and the black blotches cover his body irregularly and usually develop cancer.

Buy all of your equipment at one time. You will certainly need an aquarium, hood, heater, pump, filter, book, thermometer, airstone, three-way valve and tubing, plus gravel and plants.

There are several reasons for obtaining an aquarium this size, though to you it may look like a suitable container in which to bathe the baby. One reason is that it will hold more of the little glittering finned gems that will take your eye. It also will provide a larger water surface for the absorption of oxygen and the elimination of carbon dioxide, and it will be much easier to decorate in a pleasing way. A tank of this size also requires much less maintenance. In short, your fish will enjoy a healthier existence in a roomy tank and you will need to make fewer trips to the neighborhood drug store for aspirin.

2  *Hoods*

If you have heeded the admonition to "buy at least a 10 gallon tank," after having written it at least 100 times, you are now ready to purchase a covering for this tank. This cover is known as a "hood" or "canopy," when you are speaking the lingo of the dyed-in-the-wool aquarist.

Full hoods are available with either fluorescent or incandescent bulbs. Pictured at left below are a fluorescent full hood and several types of fluorescent bulbs; both fluorescent and incandescent bulbs are available at most pet shops. The photo at right below shows the full hood being placed into position on the tank.

This is the common Platy or "Moon" as it is sometimes called. Compare this with a Hifin Platy illustrated below. Photo by Dr. J. Norton.

A fancy Lyretail Guppy. This fish is not related to the Lyretail Molly.
Photo by Hansen.

Dr. Norton has produced this Hifin Wagtail Platy. This is a gold variety. Note
the black in *all* the fins.

A hood can take two different forms. One type of hood is called a "strip" hood, and, as its name implies, it covers only a "strip" of the surface of the aquarium, usually the front portion. The remainder is covered by a suitably cut piece of glass, that is also sometimes called a "cover glass."

A full hood made of a molded plastic is often preferable to a glass cover used with a strip reflector. The full hoods are safer. Children, for instance, often cause accidents with glass covers.

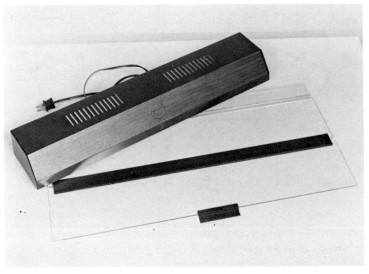

The other type of hood is a "full" hood which covers the entire tank. An aquarium *must* be covered by some sort of device, if only a piece of glass. A covering cuts down the rate of water evaporation and prohibits the more adventuresome fish, bent on seeing the other side of the mountain, from leaping out of the tank. Even some of the more stay-at-home types can be put into orbit by a slamming door, a sudden loud noise, or vibrations of any type.

3 Seeing The Light

A hood also provides illumination which your plants will need in order to flourish. Plants utilize the carbon dioxide and give off oxygen in a process called *photosynthesis,* but this is possible only when a source of good light is available. It is true that natural light can be used for this purpose, but such light is hard to control since it does not come with a handy little switch for snapping it on and off.

The strip reflectors using incandescent bulbs are often used on smaller aquariums. This type of lighting does not lend itself to a large aquarium, as fluorescent bulbs will show your fish off better . . . and they also use less electricity.

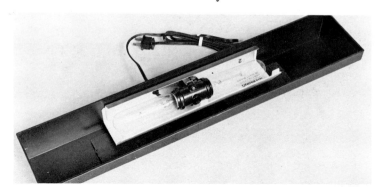

The Leopard Danio, *Brachydanio frankei*, is probably not a natural species, but is the result of a hybrid. They are excellent fish for the beginner.

Bleeding Heart Platies, above, are livebearers. The Bleeding Heart Tetras, below, are egglayers and are not related to the Platies. They get their name from the red markings near the heart.

How Green Is My Algae

4

If a little is good, a lot is not better when this statement is applied to the amount of light that you give your tank. One of the best danger signals of the fact that you have erred on the side of being over-generous with light will be an ever increasing pale green film that will start at the top of the front of your aquarium. This is because your light is usually in this place and the microscopic algae plants adore this surplus of illumination. If the over-abundance of light is not checked, before long you will have all of your rocks and plants wearing neat fuzzy little green overcoats of algae. This is not only unsightly but detrimental to your plants as well.

With a little practice the correct amount of light can be gauged so that your plants will flourish, but won't be donning their little green overcoats. A total of 60 watts in a 15 gallon tank, burning for eight hours is usually optimum and other size tanks can be scaled proportionately.

Two types of scrapers are available to keep your glass clean. The sponge type is merely a cellulose sponge on the end of a stick. The 4-in-1 scraper has a razor blade, planting tong and plastic scraper all in one unit.

Should algae develop on the sides of your tank temporarily, it can be removed with one of the handy algae scrapers that are available in most shops. Algae on plant leaves can often be removed by carefully running the leaves between your fingers or by gently rubbing with a soft cloth. Make sure, naturally, that this cloth is completely free of soap, detergent, dye or dirt.

5

The Heat's On!

And it certainly should be on in your aquarium, especially in the winter months. Remember these are "tropical" fish you are keeping and as the name implies, they need warm balmy water to keep them in optimum condition.

As a rule most tropicals do best if kept in water heated between 70° and 75°. Although some fish can stand temperatures slightly lower and others much higher, for the pink of condition the average tropical fish will do beautifully within this temperature range. The metabolism of a fish is speeded up in proportion to a rise in temperature, and this often will affect and shorten its life span.

Since most houses are not thermostatically controlled the year around, to keep an aquarium within the 70°-75° range, it is necessary to provide a method of heating the water. This is accomplished by means of special aquarium heaters and thermostats. There are many types available to hobbyists. Some have the heater and thermostat combined into one unit. Others have a separate heater and thermostat. Some heaters are submersible while others can be glued to the back glass.

Whichever model you choose, the cost of operation is reckoned in pennies. In selecting the correct wattage it should be remembered that two watts of current is necessary in order to heat a gallon of water five degrees above the temperature of the room.

Submersible heaters (example shown on right) can be placed out of view in the aquarium. Hanging heaters must be attached to the upper rim of the aquarium; they can be disguised by a heavy planting in front of the heater.

Sumatra or Tiger Barbs are active fish. They should be kept in schools to get the best effect.

6  *Keep It Clean!*

You will want to keep the water of your aquarium clean and clear. Otherwise you will see your fish only when they decide to place their little noses against the glass.

Clarity and cleanliness are accomplished by the use of filters, and in this field you will have a large choice. Basically, there are three types of filters—undergravel, inside, and outside.

The undergravel filter, as the name implies, is a filter of varying construction, usually utilizing an arrangement of plastic plates underneath the surface of the sand as filtering media.

As the name implies, undergravel filters are placed beneath a layer of gravel. These efficient filters take up little space in the aquarium.

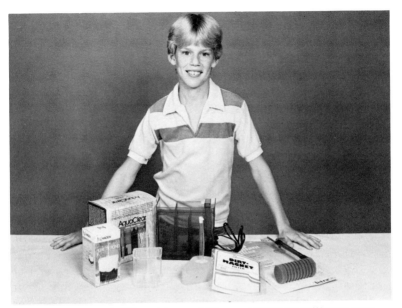

Shown are several different types of filters available for setting up your aquarium. Pictured are a corner filter, outside power filter, and two types of sponge filters.

The inside filter resembles a small plastic box. This filter is filled with charcoal and glass or Dacron wool and placed inside the tank.

Type three, the outside filter, is normally hung on the back of the tank. It, too, uses charcoal and glass or Dacron wool to remove unwanted particles from the aquarium.

With both the inside and outside filters, approximately two inches of charcoal is added first and then a wad of the wool is inserted loosely. In preparing a filter, remember to leave plenty of room for the collection of dirt that will accumulate.

Inside and outside filters should be taken apart at least once a week and cleaned for best performance. Replace the wool and charcoal regularly. Do not use the wool again and again as it harbors bacteria which may cloud your aquarium.

Some very fancy varieties of Platies have been developed. The Red Saddle Platy above has recently been developed with a Hifin (below). These live-bearer crosses are relatively easy to make by putting the male of one variety with a female of the other. Since Platies have the power of holding sperm from previous matings, don't expect results with the first mating of a non-virgin female.

These Comet Platies are very popular. By intensive inbreeding, Dr. Myron Gordon was able to produce the wagtail varieties of Swordtails and Platies. Swordtails and Platies are very closely related and can easily be crossed to one another. Random matings usually produce very poor quality fishes, but they are interesting and can produce a new variety if you carefully select the new colors and interbreed them.

Give 'Em The Air

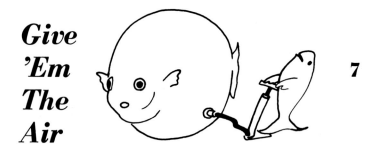

7

Aeration of your aquarium can best be accomplished by the use of an aerator or air stone. Contrary to popular belief, this device does not put oxygen into the tank, but it does effectively remove the unwanted carbon dioxide.

Aerators run from Plain Jane ones which are naked, unadorned air stones, to fancier types that blow little bubbles in all sorts of ornate ways. The selection of an aerator boils down to the effect you are striving to achieve.

If an inside or undergravel filter is used there is no need for another aerator. The bubbles arising from the filter stem will provide all that is needed in the way of aeration.

Action ornaments such as those shown serve a dual purpose: they aerate the aquarium while decorating it.

8

Pumping For Information

In order to run both filter and/or aerator you must obtain a pump. But before purchasing a pump you should acquire some information on the various models available.

Several types of air pumps are available as well as different sizes for pumping as much air as is needed. The pumps shown are all of the vibrator type.

Essentially, most pumps are of two kinds—piston or vibrator. Your dealer has a wide selection of both, geared to your needs, be they concerned with a single aquarium or a whole bank of tanks. When purchasing your first pump, look to the future. Although aquariums are admittedly inanimate objects, they do have a way of reproducing at an amazing rate. This fact may puzzle scientists, but not aquarists, who soon find that they need "just one more."

Though plastic plants are fine for beginners, there is no real substitute for the beauty of a lush, fully grown tank full of aquarium plants. This aquarium is perfectly planted with the taller plants in the rear and the shorter plants in the foreground. It is only with a careful selection of plants that do not require pruning and replanting that such a lush growth can be accomplished. It takes at least one year for a dense growth to develop. Photo by van Raam.

An excellent plant for the beginner, and one which doesn't grow too quickly, is this *Cryptocoryne willisii*.

Your local pet shop will offer all of the necessities for your aquarium all packaged together in the form of a starter kit. Included here are a heater, air pump, tubing, thermometer, air stone, gang valve, undergravel filter, net and book.

The pump is connected to the aerator and/or filter by means of plastic tubing. Air is controlled through one three-way valve for each filter or aerator used, plus one end valve for the entire hook-up. Should there be too much air, any excess can then "bleed" off through the end valve.

Plastic valves have the advantage of being less expensive, less heavy and more rust-proof than metal valves. Brass valves are poisonous if immersed in the aquarium.

9 **Wall To Wall Gravel**

Flooring or "carpeting" in the little glass house of your new fishy pets should be sand or gravel. This also provides the planting medium for the flora of your aquarium.

Take the middle ground here and buy gravel that is neither too fine nor too coarse. If it's too fine the roots of the plants will have difficulty probing through it as it becomes packed. If it's too coarse, minute food particles will get down in the crevices, out of reach of even the busiest little scavengers. No. 3 gravel in natural color is most commonly used and is quite satisfactory. However, interesting and colorful effects can be obtained by using some of the kaleidoscopic hues of the colored gravels.

In figuring the amount of sand needed, a good rule of thumb is two pounds to a gallon. Most of the gravel available in pet shops is pre-washed, but it does no harm to wash it once again. This can best be done by placing it in a large container, such as a bucket, and running a strong stream of water down through it, agitating the gravel with your hand until the water runs clear. A container selected for use with your fish should never be used for any other purpose. Never put a detergent in it, since an infinitesimal amount can prove fatal to fish. This also is true of a slight amount left clinging to your hands. Rinse them carefully of detergent or soap before putting them into your fish tanks.

Rocking Your Aquarium  10

Decorative rocks could be termed the "furniture" you'll place on your gravel carpet. They add much eye appeal and interest to a tank. Although you may have some unique or oddly formed rocks picked up on hikes at the beach, it is best to purchase your rocks from your dealer. Then you can be absolutely certain that you will not be introducing materials containing harmful minerals into your aquarium. Petrified wood in its many variations makes excellent "furniture" for your fishes because of its completely natural appearance.

Petrified wood, *"Si!"* Natural wood, *"No!"* If you see an especially interesting piece of gnarled knotted wood, you

Another excellent plant which doesn't require too much light is *Cryptocoryne nevillii*.

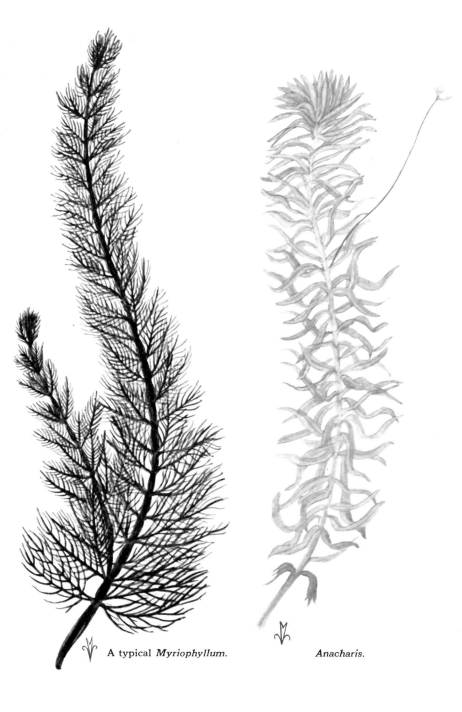

A typical *Myriophyllum*.

Anacharis.

Backgrounds that can be taped to the back of the aquarium are designed
with natural scenes.

may be tempted to include it in your tank to add to the natural appearance. It is best to squelch this impulse, however, and rely on odd manzanita branches that your dealer will often have on hand, if you feel that you must have some type of wood in your tank. These branches are treated and safe for submersion in water.

How Does Your Garden Grow?

11

The plants that you select for your aquarium will be a small garden through which your fish will swim. Here you will appreciate one of the first delights of fish-keeping, for there are many beautiful plants to delight the eye.

Select plants that will complement your fish and act as a background in displaying their colors. Do not obscure the fish any more than is absolutely necessary. The tall plants should be placed in the rear of the tank and graduate in size until at the very front you will have the pygmy and dwarf varieties.

One of the most commonly used plants of the taller varieties for background planting is *Vallisneria*. Any of the varieties of this popular plant will enhance a tank with its green ribbon-like leaves.

Sagittaria is another old "work horse" of the aquarium. Its leaves are similar to *Vallisneria*, but heavier in character. The dwarf varieties of this plant make excellent foreground material.

Other stand-bys are the many varieties of *Cryptocoryne*. It almost seems as if nature has produced a type of *Crypt* to suit every purpose. They are very satisfactory plants for beginners and can provide a nice color contrast, since some of the varieties have a reddish cast to the leaves.

Rock forms molded from plastic can be snapped together to form caves,
walls, rock bridges, or mounds.

Plants in the aquarium provide your fishes with hiding places while adding to the attractiveness of the set-up.

Use these sketches to plan your own aquarium decor.

Breeding tanks for live-bearers should be fairly densely planted with many floating plants.

For fishes that swim on the top of the water, like Swordtails, use plants which leave the top of the tank free.

For maximum enjoyment of a community aquarium, keep the center front of the aquarium open.

For use as "baby-hiders" when the small livebearers come into the world, floating plants such as *Myriophyllum* or *Ceratophyllum demersum* (hornwort) are excellent, and a sturdy bunch plant such as *Hygrophila* has many uses.

There are numerous varieties of plants available to the aquarist, as any trip to a dealer will attest. Only a small sampling has been mentioned. It is best not to go overboard in your selection, however. Three or four varieties are much more pleasing in an average tank than a dozen or more, no matter how attractive each plant may be.

Plants aren't just decorative; they are utilitarian as well. Not only do they convert carbon dioxide given off by the fish into oxygen, they also utilize the fish detritus as fertilizer and attractively give the fish a green, leafy security.

Although the plants you purchase may look similar to land flora, they do have different requirements. One of the major ones is the method of planting. So forget that shovel. Instead, the plant should be taken carefully in one hand and inserted in the gravel a few inches from the place where the plant ultimately is to reside. It is then pushed through the gravel to the desired spot, as you efficiently bury the fine rootlets and anchor the plant in place. Otherwise, you run the risk of having small pale roots waving around in the current, looking for all the world like the small ghosts of departed snakes.

Lately, new plastic plants have appeared on the aquarium scene. Many are almost exact copies of real, live, natural aquarium plants...but most are colorful items which make the aquarium a more beautiful and interesting addition to the household. The idealist would never dream of having anything artificial in his aquarium; but millions of plastic aquarium plants are sold each and every year, so there is no use in fighting the fad. If used properly they are ornamental and the fish seem to like them almost as much as the real thing.

These magnificent Hifin Swordtails with lyretails were raised and photographed by Mr. Glenn Takeshita in Hawaii.

Black Tetras are very popular fishes and easy to care for. The Black Neon (below) will live in most aquariums but it does better in slightly acid water with a pH of 6.4.

12 Piscine Potpourri

You'll soon find a multitude of other equipment completely indispensible before you have been in the hobby very long. Some of these will include siphon hoses, feeding rings, algae scrapers, or various other cleaning devices, nets, and thermometers. Keeping fish is like raising a baby. You'll find that it takes much equipment to efficiently maintain one very small living organism.

13 Setting Up Exercises

With everything in readiness, you can now embark on setting up all of your equipment into an integrated whole —your glass-encased special bit of tropical river.

First of all, your tank must be placed on a firm, unyielding surface. Keep in mind that each gallon of water weighs more than eight pounds. Secondly, add the undergravel filter, if you are using such a piece of equipment; otherwise pour the gravel or sand into place. Slope the gravel gently from the back of the tank down to two or three inches at the front. You will have better viewing of your fish and also will make it easy to siphon off any foreign matter that might accumulate.

It is now time to call upon your artistic talents and place your rocks where you will. When everything meets with your approval, place a piece of newspaper, wrapping paper, or plastic over the top of your arrangement. Carefully pour your water on this surface. This will keep the gravel from washing out of place.

If an outside filter is used, add it at any time. If an inside filter is your desire, it can be added at the time the

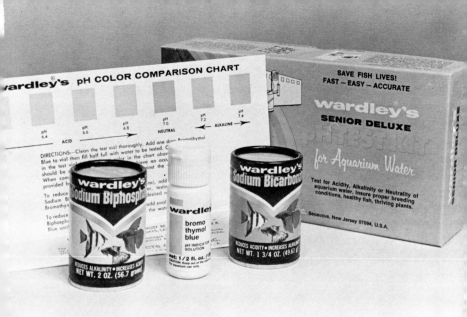

Every complete aquarium setup should have auxiliary equipment to make fishkeeping simpler. A "water laboratory" is necessary, not only to measure the pH, but to adjust it as well.

Cleaning the aquarium is an important part of fish-keeping. A gravel cleaner (left) helps you remove waste that has settled in the gravel. The aquarium siphon is helpful when making partial water changes.

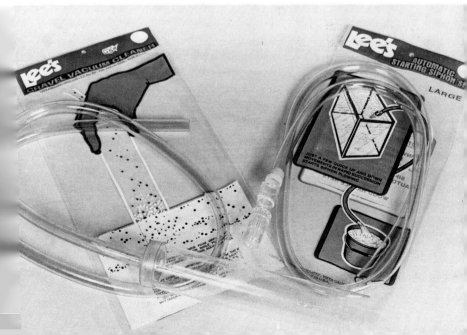

rocks are put in and usually can be concealed behind one. The same procedure is followed for thermostats and heaters, depending upon whether they hang over the back of the inside of the aquarium or are to be concealed as submersible ones in the rear of the tank.

Fill the tank with water to approximately three inches from the top. This will allow you to put your hands inside the tank to arrange your plants without spilling any water over the sides like a miniature Niagara Falls. Always remember to insert the roots a few inches from their ultimate resting spot, and then move them toward their goal.

When the planting has been completed to your satisfaction, the tank can be filled the rest of the way. Ideally, the water should be allowed to age overnight. This allows it to rise to the desired temperature and any chlorine, which is added by many water companies, is dissipated.

Before you bring home your fishes, check the pH of the water with a pH Test Kit. Then check the pH of the water in the store from which you bought the fishes. If the pH is different you will have to slowly adjust the water so the water is the same. Talk to your dealer about the problem and he'll suggest how to remedy it.

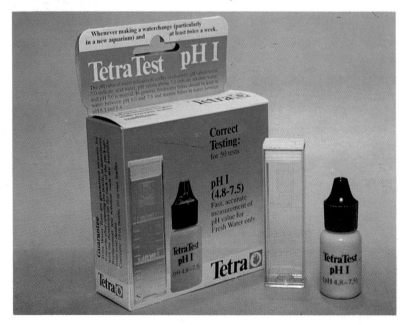

Siamese Fighting Fish, *Betta splendens,* are very popular aquarium fish. You can only keep one male in an aquarium since more than one will fight. This variety, with fins longer than its body, is the Libby Betta. It comes in almost every color you can imagine including red, blue, green, pink, white and dark purple.

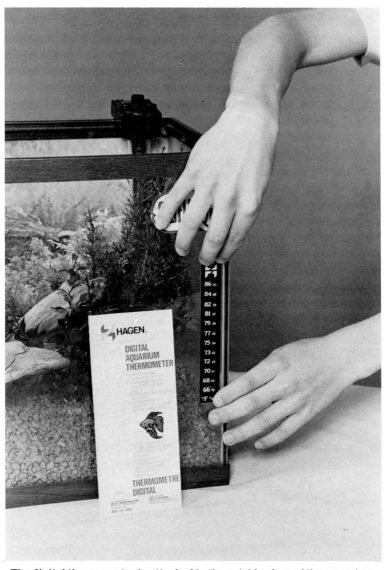

The digital thermometer is attached to the outside glass of the aquarium. Digital thermometers are highly accurate.

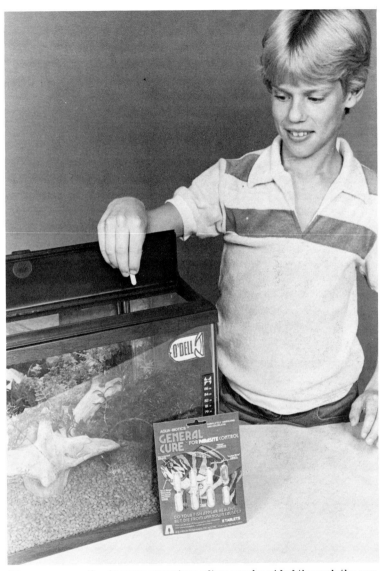

Disease prevention in your aquarium often can be aided through the use of a general cure or remedy on a regular basis.

The Glowlight Tetra from South America is so named because of the beautiful
red line running through its body. Another beautiful and inexpensive fish is the
Flame Tetra, also from South America (below).

From Thailand comes the Redtailed Black Shark. This is not a true shark. It gets its name from the shark-like dorsal fin. One of the best scavengers for the aquarium is the Plecostomus (below) from Trinidad and almost every other country in South America.

Fish take a very black view of chlorine—in fact, they look upon it as deadly poison. This may be why you run into very few Guppies in swimming pools.

If it is not possible to age your water before adding your fish, one of the chlorine-removal chemicals should be added. These are available in any shop where tropical fish supplies are sold.

It is absolutely essential that the temperature of the water in the little plastic bag in which your fish are residing when they come home from the store is identical to the temperature of their new glass house. To accomplish this, the unopened bag should be floated in the tank until a thermometer proclaims that the water in the two containers is the same degree.

When you get right down to it, fish are rather a stuffy lot. They don't cotton to extreme temperature plunges in either direction and it's best to go along with them on this point. If you don't they have a way of getting even with you—they get sick and die.

Check the pH of your water, too. It should be close to that which your pet shop uses. Simple pH kits are available at the pet shop where you bought your fish.

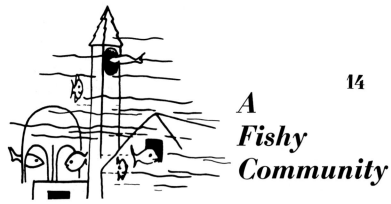

14

A
Fishy
Community

You are now ready for the inhabitants of your little piece of tropical river. Your aquarium is, of course, a small community, the inhabitants of which must all live together in peace and harmony if it is to be a success.

The ideal members, and hence the more successful fish for a beginner, include, first of all the Livebearers, so named because their babies are born alive. Any of the many color variations of Guppies, Platies, Swordtails, and Mollies make fine community fish as a rule.

The remainder of tropical fish fall into the general category of egg layers. A random selection of fish that fit the "ideal community tank citizen" label are Dwarf Gouramis, Kissing Gouramis, Pearl Gouramis, Neon Tetras, Head and Tail-lights, Glo-lite Tetras, Serpaes, Bleeding Heart Tetras, Black Tetras, Cardinal Tetras, *Rasbora heteromorpha*, Angels of one variety or another, Zebras, and Pearl Danios. One male Betta also can be included, but more than one is disastrous. They will destroy each other.

There are many tropical fish from which to make a selection, but a few taken from this cross section will do well. At least two of each kind, with the exception of the Bettas, should be purchased. Because of a natural tendency in tropical fish to "school," they feel more secure with at least one other of their kind in the tank.

At the bottom of the list, only because they are found on the bottom of most tanks, are the little catfish. At least two of the little *Corydoras* species should be included. *Corydoras* are the most common catfish and the least expensive. These are the little clean-up crews with the five o'clock shadow. They diligently poke their little whiskers into each and every cranny to ferret out forgotten food particles, thus preventing a foul tank.

Another scavenger, the snail, also can be included but he often presents a mixed blessing. Snails sometimes get confused and eat the plants right along with the discarded food and algae.

A knotty problem is, "How many fish does a tank hold?" An ancient axiom says, "One inch of fish to a gallon," but one should err on the side of too few fish rather than too many. Fish are always competing for the available oxygen in an aquarium. When there isn't enough to go around, the weaker fish will die first.

Feed your fishes regularly. By buying Freeze Dried Tubifex Worms you can stick a piece onto the glass and enjoy watching your fishes tear pieces from it. This is ideal for the beginner who should be sure he doesn't overfeed his fishes. Remove uneaten food after fifteen minutes.

15

Feeding the Multitude

Fish, like people, prefer to eat regularly, but this doesn't mean three squares a day. One meal is sufficient, although smaller night and morning feedings are possible. Before beginning to feed your fish look at them closely. Notice what little space in their bodies the internal organs

Cardinal Tetras, *Cheirodon axelrodi,* are the most popular of all fishes and millions are sold every year. These fish are feasting on Freeze Dried Tubifex worms.

take up. Keep this in mind and you'll never be guilty of the cardinal sin of fish keeping—*over feeding*.

Lean toward the side of starving your fish until you can gauge what they will completely clean up within a 15 minute period. Uneaten food will deteriorate and promote bacterial growth detrimental to all inhabitants of the aquarium.

The most common food of tropicals is dry food. All of the fish listed in Chapter 14 will eat it, with the exception of the *Betta*. Sometimes *Bettas* will eat it too, but they need a diet predominantly rich in live food. Always take the advice of your dealer. If he says that a certain fish will eat nothing but live food, don't buy that fish unless you intend to feed live food.

There is a vast array of dry food on the market so don't stick with one kind. Rotate two or three varieties for best results. You wouldn't like to sit down to a meal of liver and onions day in and day out, and your fish appreciate variety too.

All fish, even if they dote on dry food, relish a little live food now and then. This comes in the form of either frozen food or food "on the hoof." Frozen varieties include daphnia (a small red water flea) and brine shrimp (a small crustacean whose lot in life seems to be destined as a blue plate special for fish.) These foods come in small compact packages at your dealers. They easily can be shaved off with a sharp knife for daily portions.

A popular squirming and wiggling live food—*Tubifex* —look like miniature angleworms. Keep them cool in a small amount of water in your refrigerator. *Daphnia* and brine shrimp are often obtainable in live forms. When you become more advanced and adventurous and raise your own live food, get a "start" of white worms from your pet shop.

Freeze dried Tubifex are also excellent, and have the added advantage of being "sticky." A dried cube is pressed into position on the inside front glass. The fish usually attack it vigorously, thus affording you the opportunity of viewing your fishes upon command. It is simple to use Freeze-Dried Tubifex for fish-training purposes.

16  *Peaked Pisces*

As with human ills, that old saw, "One ounce of prevention is worth a pound of cure" cuts a lot of wood here, too. And one of the best ounces of prevention that you can get is to quarantine any new fish that you buy for several days in "solitary" before adding them to the rest of the crew. This way, any unnoted disease can be isolated before it has a chance to spread and can thus be contained.

A second "ounce of prevention" consists of checking over your fish, plants and gravel regularly with an eagle eye. Do your fish carry their little fins bolt upright and do they swim around in a sassy, eager manner? Or are their fins clamped to the sides of their bodies and they are "swimming" without going anywhere? Are your plants flourishing? Or are they yellowing on their way to sickening and dying? Smell your tank when you raise the hood—is there a good fresh healthy "fishy" smell about it? Or is there a "hold your nose" quality about it? Before long you'll be able to recognize the healthy smell of an aquarium that bodes vibrant good health for your little charges.

Even with the best possible care an ailment may befall your fish. Chilling probably is the greatest enemy of your fish, since this lowers their resistance to disease.

The most common disease of tropicals is something by the jaw-snapping name of *Ichthyophthirius.* If aquarists had to pronounce it correctly before curing it, there would be few fish around. Fortunately, this wretched disease simply is known by the monicker of "Ick." Imagine how a fish would look if someone stood five paces away and hurled a handful of sugar at it. Some white crystals would stick to the fish. This is what the nasty little parasite called "Ick" looks like. A number of preparations are on the market to eradicate it. The most beneficial cures contain

The red nose on this fish is not a sickness, it is the Rummy-nose Tetra from South America. The fish below is not so lucky. This Mickey Mouse Platy (so named for the pattern on the caudal peduncle) with the hifin has Ich. Look closely and you can see the small white spots which characterize this disease.

One of the hardiest fishes for beginners is the White Cloud Mountain Fish from China. They are easy to breed. Try them in an aquarium all by themselves.

malachite green or acriflavine. This remedy, coupled with raising the temperature to 85° usually is effective.

If Ick is allowed to go untreated your fish will develop a fungus which looks like puffs of cotton attached to it. While Ick is due to a small animal, fungus is due to a microscopic plant. Both are parasitic in nature. Often fungus will come from an injury when the natural slimy protective coating of your fish is disturbed, if, for example, it leaps out of the tank. It is important to pick up your fish with wet hands or a wet net.

Numerous commercial preparations are on the market for fungus. Some of them are beneficial for Ick. Whichever brand you choose, be sure to follow the manufacturer's instructions exactly. If a little is good, a lot is not better in treating tropical fish.

Diseases other than the two most common ones also can attack your fish. Some of them are treatable. It is best to consult with your fish dealer when a strange illness strikes one of your fishy family. He or she is the best person to consult for remedies and reassurance. Before you dally long in the tropical fish hobby you'll come to regard your pet dealer almost as heroically as you do your family doctor.

Roll Over And Play Dead

17

Having learned the ground rules for keeping your fish fit and happy, perhaps you've got a minute or two that hangs heavy on your hands. For fun, try "educating" your small charges a little.

Its easy to train fishes to eat from your hand with Freeze Dried Tubifex worms. This catfish, normally very timid, eagerly eats large chunks.

The Rasbora, a very popular fish, comes from Singapore. The fishes below are a mixed group of Cardinal Tetras and Neons, both from Brazil.

There are more than thirty different species of *Corydoras*. They make excellent scavengers, always poking about on the bottom of the tank. The fish below is a beautiful Veiltail Angelfish. No community tank is complete without them.

Now constantly keep in mind that 1/50th of the body weight of a human being is represented by our brains, but only 1/720th to 1/1305th of the weight of a fish is taken up by this organ. It isn't realistic to think that you'll be able to teach your fish to sit up and beg, speak for their dinner, or even come swimming up to you with your pipe and slippers in their damp little mouths. One trick they can do with your help is to leap out of the water for food.

Since there is a great variation in the I.Q. of fishes, it is wise to pick the quiz kids of the aquarium set for any training you wish to offer. The smartest tropical fish you'll find in the average tank belong to the family Cichlidae. Of this group, the most responsive to learning is the *Astronotus ocellatus,* or "Oscar" as he is more familiarly known to his intimates. Large catfish are also easy to tame.

Here's how to teach Oscar to leap for his dinner. Props needed for this trick include one clump of freeze-dried Tubifex and one rain coat. The rain coat is for the person holding the Tubifex and the Tubifex is for Oscar. Once Oscar has learned to leap several inches out of the water for his meal and re-enter the water with a resounding splash you'll appreciate the purpose of the rain coat!

Start by holding the Dry Tubifex only an inch or two above the water. When Oscar becomes proficient at each height, raise the Dry Tubifex higher, as a pole vaulter does his bar.

A slight variation is to fasten the worms to a small tab which is attached to a bell. After a few rounds of grabbing the worms from the tab and ringing the bell in the process, a smart Oscar will catch on that the ringing of the bell might bring on dinner.

Fish do have memories and have been proven to be trainable. Evidence of a memory is seen when a glass partition kept in a tank for a long time is taken out. The fish will keep swimming in the same old rounds, not passing over the invisible bounds of the old barrier.

While conventional fish are never going to win any **Phi Beta Kappa** keys, it's a sure bet your fishy community will bring you much enjoyment.

Corydoras aeneus, above, are closely related to the *Corydoras* on page 61. This species is almost colorless. The Zebra Danios, below, come from India, but they are easily bred and are excellent for the community tank.

The Oscar, *Astronotus ocellatus,* is one of the easiest fish to tame

A pair of Honey Gouramis from India, *Colisa chuna*. Photo by Zukal.